Praise for *You and Three Others Are Approaching a Lake*

"*You and Three Others Are Approaching a Lake* is that rare book capable not only of giving its reader something new, but also of pointing out that which is so salient about our lives we no longer see it."
—H_NGM_N

"Easy-on-the-ear, accessible, wise, and funny. [. . .] She takes on the big questions by way of unusual details."
—*BOOKFORUM*

"In her second book of poetry, Anna Moschovakis presents an engaging lyric analysis of the contemporary frameworks people live within. Ideas about choice (and indecisiveness), consumption, comfort, indulgence, and the evolution of collective vocabularies are explored, using the rhetoric of Internet-speak, ethics texts, historical anecdotes, and argument."
—*AMERICAN POET*

"I didn't believe I could delight in a poetry of cultural critique until I read *You and Three Others Are Approaching a Lake*. Capitalism, clinical definitions of personhood and desire, bloodlust, waste, guilt—the four serial poems in this collection wrangle with issues so big and painful that the mind reels; yet at times I found myself laughing out loud. 'Death as a Way of Life' poses the question, 'Can a grammar kill?' If it can, I hail Anna Moschovakis as Chief of the New Poetic Army."
—DODIE BELLAMY

"Tragedy has its taxonomies—therein lies its beauty, and the beauty of *You and Three Others Are Approaching a Lake*. Like life, like poetry, like the reworking of the happenstance of language and the random facticity of human eloquence and violence, Moschovakis's pieces cut into and through the fact of what matters. Like a child's cry."
—VANESSA PLACE

The James Laughlin Award is given to recognize and support a poet's second book. It is the only second-book award for poetry in the United States. Offered since 1954, the award was endowed in 1995 by a gift to the Academy from the Drue Heinz Trust. It is named for the poet and publisher James Laughlin (1914–1997), who founded New Directions in 1936.

YOU AND THREE OTHERS ARE APPROACHING A LAKE

YOU AND THREE OTHERS ARE APPROACHING A LAKE

Anna Moschovakis

COFFEE HOUSE PRESS

MINNEAPOLIS

2011

Coffee House Press books are available to the trade through our pri-
mary distributor, Consortium Book Sales & Distribution,
www.cbsd.com or (800) 283-3572. For personal orders, catalogs, or
other information, write to: info@coffeehousepress.org.

    Coffee House Press is a nonprofit literary publishing house.
Support from private foundations, corporate giving programs, gov-
ernment programs, and generous individuals helps make the publica-
tion of our books possible. We gratefully acknowledge their support
in detail in the back of this book.

To you and our many readers around the world,
we send our thanks for your continuing support.

LIBRARY OF CONGRESS CIP INFORMATION

Moschovakis, Anna.
You and three others are approaching a lake / Anna Moschovakis. — 1st ed.
p. cm.
Poems, some of which have appeared or been excerpted in other publications.
ISBN 978-1-56689-250-6 (ALK. PAPER)
I. Title.
PS3613.O7787Y68 2010
811'.6—DC22
2010016459

PRINTED IN THE UNITED STATES

1 3 5 7 9 8 6 4

Systems about fact must plunge themselves into sensation
as bridges plunge their piers into the rock.

—WILLIAM JAMES

"the senses have their own nature, and therefore
    cannot disclose absolute truth—

"The mind has ~~an inherent logic~~ ^its own nature^, and therefore
    supplies necessary truth"   a double standard.

—GEORGE OPPEN

[prologue]

The problem is I don't care whether I convince you or not
In a perfect world I would be able to convince you of this

Everybody should always have a position on everything
We take our positions with us, like folding stools to the beach
The stools, when we abandon them, fade to the same color

And I will go with you to the end of this argument
As I have gone with you to the beach
And the man with the cooler will walk by selling streets
And we will pick a street to carry us home

We'll pick the one with the best-loved name
A flower or a state or October the 12th
Because each date must be celebrated somewhere in this world
Each moment of courage or loss or revolution
When something pushed something and something fell down

THE TRAGEDY OF WASTE

You and three others are approaching a lake
You have two canoes, your tent, your axes
It is after six
What, precisely, is your procedure?

      To be fed
      To keep warm and dry

One had brought back poisonous toadstools
One had lain down on the beach
Had cut down tall trees for—

We start not with theory but with tangible performance
Enter: the world,
a species already
sufficiently inured to tragedy

At the beginning of 1917 there were housewives
children, old people, sick people
fields, factories, stores, offices
food, shelter, and clothing

Modern industrialism
the slums of the great cities
reasonable comforts

We entered with 40,000,000 workers
warriors
uniforms and boots

We made graphs
were surprised on the home front:

The house went up faster with three men
than with four

What miracle occurred?
No miracle.

You are approaching a lake. You have canoes, tent, axes.

The heroine says: *We shall first try to secure*
an aeroplane view of our own

This taxes the imagination. Too many studies have begun
and ended in the middle.

The businessman is beginning to think
The engineer knows it   the good

                                republican knows it

From these definitions one must pick
and choose

You are plunged into a field
a quiet, celestial eyesight
an aeroplane view

Suppose that Mr. David Friday and
Sir Leo Chiozza Money
had had their way

      flickered for a moment
      and then went out
     "under the cold douche"

Suppose that instead of killing Germans
the organization had been directed
to the killing of malnutrition, slum dwelling,
shoddy clothing, infant mortality, occupational disease, starved
opportunity, illiteracy, and ignorance

     for example

This plunges us into a field
some 100,000,000 men, women, and children
in relation to these things

What are those 600,000 people in the advertising business up to,
    for instance?
A housewife tries to get her chores done in the morning
so she can go to a matinee in the afternoon

With these principles in mind,
set down as waste:

the production of nonessentials, idleness, bad
technical methods

(the case of the camping party on page one, the poisonous
toadstools, the beach)

There are five elements involved in the theory
and we will consider each of them briefly:

Human wants
(   )

Wastes in consumption
(   )

Idle manpower
(   )

Wastes in the technique of production and distribution
(   )

The waste of natural resources
(   )

Human wants:

First the necklace of bone
then the shift of leather

tea, tobacco, and gambling

in other words

ten men could live on the corn
where only one can live on the beef

Wastes in consumption, or illth:

It has been said (following Ruskin) that

"The production of base forms of art in painting, music, the drama, literature, the plastic arts, must necessarily entail the highest human costs, the largest loss of human welfare, individual and social. For such an artist poisons not only his own soul but the social soul, adulterating the food designed to nourish the highest faculties of man."

In other words:

> Language: it is fun to watch
> but it is even more fun to play

or

> More than 2,000 persons have been killed in theater collapses
> in the past ten years

or

> Adulteration packed the life preservers of the *General Slocum*
> with sawdust instead of cork
> as she sank with all on board

More illth:

We are not concerned with who pays for it
but with the thing itself

If it is a beautiful thing
It is not waste

But outside the field of art

a pile of sound comforts and
a pile of wanton extravagance

(two canoes, your axes)

I would like an explanation of these canoes and axes. Someone, somewhere is approaching. There is a lake, the concept of supply and demand, a war with which to compete. Who among you will not use the axe? Who will forsake the lake?

It's been said:

> A functional society would not abolish
> sexual irregularities
> and could not
> if it would

of course

law of difference, law
of diminishing

return, or

The lake does not have to be the next last stop

Did you ever think you could
stay where you are, irregular

The canoe turned over is
a house

Idle manpower:

From the aeroplane view it was noted
that certain adults were doing nothing

Men are not idle because they want to be
We cannot always be successful

Because he dislikes his job,
the total
the United States . . .

They are temporarily laid off
seasonally laid off
cyclically laid off

They are out of work for an average period

As they change from job to job

      needless

      agony

You have your tent, your canoes,
a species already—

Wastes in production:

In the war, all this was beginning to change

the belting
the power load
the lubricating and cooling devices
the handling of supplies
and the physical motions of the men who run the tools

what pain is to a human
body

the most efficient machine

In the printing industry
there is only one apprentice
for every ten journeyman printers

a condition the engineers term
"Industrial suicide"

    example:

    example:

    example:

We confess it is with sorrow
that we see a child enter
upon this desert

An analysis of advertising:

Ride on trains
Stay at home more
Use more coffins!

Eat more bread
Drink more milk
Eat more butter
Eat more cheese

Eat more meat (Goal: 179 lbs. per capita per year, the level
attained in 1900)

The eye is caught, and often it is pleased

We must pick and choose:

smiling faces, shining teeth, schoolgirl complexions, cornless feet,
perfect-fitting union suits, distinguished collars, wrinkleless pants,
odorless breaths, regularized bowels, happy homes in New Jersey
(15 minutes from Hoboken), charging motors, punctureless tires,
perfect busts, shimmering shanks, self-washing dishes . . . backs
behind which the moon was meant to rise!

Industrial co-ordination (star-crossed love):

Finally, he arose
and said:

"These great varieties of styles to choose from
do not reflect the wishes of the consumer

In the resulting gulf, untold men and women
submerged and lost

Through failure

    (ignorance of supply and demand
    the seasonal cycle of rush months
    and dull months

    uncertain sales, uncertain
    sources)

We could go on indefinitely

No personal stricture is possible
Put it out of reach

naïve intelligence of a boy

I will confess . . ."

Wastes in distribution:

Is he?
How much?
Has it?

Well then, we'll smash it!

There is no internal price system
Mother does not charge for frying eggs
nor Father for shaking down
the furnace

Behind the desk there is a window

A woodpecker is attacking the house
The sun is attacking the snow on the pavement

Everything helping itself
to everything else

Natural resources (the gutting of a continent):

You and three others are approaching a lake
The day of the pioneer may have passed its noon
but it still runs strong

It is after six. What is your procedure?

The history of the material conquest
of America largely parallels

the history of every other
rich and virgin area

Free experimentation, trial and error
No job for academic philosophers

Those hunters who slew bird and lynx
as their stomachs and their safety demanded—

is it more than you would have done?

The error is material—it's an island ahead. You are already in the lake.

*An oil well is a hole in the ground about a quarter of a mile deep
into which a man may put a small fortune
or out of which he make take a big one.*

There were housewives, children,
shelter and clothing

reasonable comforts

The island turned over
is a canoe

The challenge: to start
not with theory but with tangible performance

You and others, approaching

We shall be asked for a way out

        to be fed

        to keep warm and dry

Starting with experience, magic
genuine science

More than once we have been lost
in a trackless wilderness

dwarfed and shadowed by mighty buildings
subway trains wild as elephants

One goes blindly back to one's desk

These moments come, their dark
shadow

We glimpsed control
and more tragic waste

We entered with 40,000,000 warriors
with the dignity of cathedrals

The lake is upon you.
You have two canoes, your tent
The child has entered upon this desert

You have your axes

What, precisely, is your procedure?

DEATH AS A WAY OF LIFE

It began:

1. Life is not fair
2. How can I be happy while others suffer
3. How can I not be happy while others suffer
4. Others will suffer whether or not I am happy
5. It is not the suffering of others that causes my happiness
6. It is not the not-suffering of others that causes my unhappiness
7. The not-suffering of others would not prevent my happiness
8.

I have been attracted to the idea that naming is a form of violence
but does that mean we should go around calling everyone *Hey You*
which seems like another sort of violence
even though it is a way of recognizing the other
as other

What can be said on this point?

—

Ancient man, and we have ample evidence of this,
used to drive whole herds of animals over
cliffs when the individual beasts were too formidable
or too fast to handle

an admirable technique
with a dubious result

In 1755 Louis xv
assembled 13 hunters
for an 18-day excursion

Among them was a woman
Princess Charlotte
who fired 9,010 shots
to the king's thousand

They returned with:
19 stags
18,243 hares
10 foxes
19,545 partridges
9,499 pheasants
114 larks
353 quail
454 "other birds"

for a total 48,237 killed

The carcasses came home in bags
the nobles came home drunk

I want to know about the "other birds"

Were they species unknown to the hunters
or insignificant birds not worth noting by name
or mutilated
beyond recognition
by the princess
an obviously staunch lady

Then there is the Jewish thinker Emmanuel Lévinas
who wrote about violence and the Other
who once made me think of Emmanuelle Béart
in her role as *La belle noiseuse,*
in which she is in the nude most of the time
an object for art
some would say violence

But think of *noiseuse*
and its origin
could be *noire*
or *nuire,* a verb meaning "hurt"
or *noise*
and its uses

When I first saw the film I thought it meant hazelnut
but the French word for hazelnut is *noisette*, and *noiseuse*
it turns out is a person who likes
to pick a fight, a gadfly

Emmanuel Lévinas was a gadfly, too
though not only when naked like Emmanuelle Béart
and he didn't have "art" in his name like she does

He didn't have "philosophy" or "ethics" either
or even, or especially, "theology"

The theologians

("The theologians" is an attractive phrase   sounds laughable but
with an underbelly   like all my subjects)

(It also reminds me that the words "theology" and "logic"   are
related by the root word, "log"   and that when I was young   a
log was a bridge that got you safely   to the other side)

Man dies in excess but not
naturally for in all his genius
he is still to find a better way
to solve his differences
than that used by his ape<—>man
ancestors

And so the log becomes a weapon
the weapon a float
to fight over

(Competition the spice of life
when I was young
I was a gadfly, too)

There are no theologians in my family
my ancestors
held by a string
to the map

—

To master death does not simply mean
to remain one's master in the face of death

Tell this to the unnamed birds
creatures of appetite
fulfilled, death's
true masters
teaching men and princesses
to be gods

Or to the nameless Flemish painter
the Master of Winter Landscapes
and his countless paintings
called *Winter Landscape*
(or *In the Face of Death*)

Or should it be
Death as a Way of Life
the title of a book
published in hardcover
the year of my birth
nineteen-hundred seventy

six years before the country
turned 200 and my brother
got stitched
in his chin

In 1970 humans are listed
as the "only major factor"
in the endangerment of
the red uakari
bald uakari
black-headed uakari
and 39 other mammals, including
the pig-tailed langur
snow leopard
and giant armadillo

But hunters are not to blame for everything

—

We wonder at our shifting capacities, keep
adding and striking skills
from the bottoms of our résumés
under constant revision
like the inscriptions on tombs
shared for generations
unnervingly up
to date

Made nervous by our shift in capabilities, we write:

> I visited a country where kittens lay dying
> under every bench, in every gutter, next to
> every cigarette butt. One made me weep.
> Two made me worry. Three made me
> look away. I visited a city with very few
> strays. The first one I saw I adopted.
> What could it mean?
> —posted by Sarah. 6.18.06

Hit "publish" and look away

The New Violence: I visited a country where
everything looked like home

—

There is a stag on the stage
played by a boy who likes
to dress like a girl. The hunter
pulls on his antlers, making him
cry. The audience explodes

There is a bomb on the stage
where the boy takes revenge,
undone, climbing the ropes to the rafters
peeing on the scrim

The hunter pisses her pants
before dying. There
is a stage on the stage
we know

My own chin was stitched
in 2004, by an Inuit girl
with bangs. A stitch in time, I thought
at her thick black braids

We know
we need to be sensitive
to the other's right to kill

Let the Inuit hunt their whales, don't

pack bumper stickers
in the boxes of baseballs

The stage is a diamond
with home in one corner,
our corner, our sliver
of heaven

I'm mad about shooting birds and animals. It's the nearest
thing to heaven, in human terms, that I know.

—Right Reverand David Cashman, Roman Catholic Bishop,
Circa MCMLXX

—

In the 1850s a seven-shot "Victoria"
revolver cost $2.50.
Victory is cheap
they say

      With seven bullets you could shoot a woman
      in both breasts, both ovaries, her vagina and clitoris
      with one bullet left for a target of choice

      Somebody may have done this
      or imagined it before

      I've imagined worse, and so have you.
                    —posted by Rick. 6.19.06

Revenge is dear. Dear reader
don't take yours now

—

Man dies, that is nothing.

but

      when a woman sits on the edge of her bed, in front of a window, and lets down her red silken hair, threading it through her delicate fingers as it cascades in waves down her porcelain back, which reflects the moon's silvery mood, so that any man privileged enough to catch a glimpse of her falls directly to his knees, blind, lost, panting for breath, choking on words he can't pronounce, starving for familiar phrases he can no longer retrieve from their world of abstraction now that *the real thing* is manifest before him, so that he vomits up his lunch, his excellent breakfast, and the previous night's dinner, disgusted with anything he saw fit to consume before setting sight on this morsel of perfection, and lies there in half-crazed ecstasy for three days and three long nights, without food or water, his senses damaged to the point of extinction, until he is on the verge of death, and the moon's high silver has fallen to dust, and nobody can help him so nobody tries, and the woman is gone, and her hair is gone, and her porcelain back is gone, and her slender fingers, and even her image is gone, and still he has no regrets, and he welcomes death, invites it, knowing as he's never known anything before that his life wants for nothing

      now *that* is something

            heaven

  a sliver

—

An interesting question to ask here, I think, concerns the nature
of sentimentality. Is the man (read: person) that says, "Take down
the gallows!" essentially the same man who says,
"Thou shalt not kill beasts for kicks"?

We don't know yet. Generally, the hunter
tends to be more pragmatic than the anti-hunter

Is the person (read: person) who sits in a chair
while another person administers an injection
that causes the first person to slump over, blind, lost, panting for breath,
and vomit up lunch, breakfast, and the previous night's dinner,
with nobody to help and nobody trying,
until death emerges as a singular desire,
the only way out of a worsening situation
a heaven of its own
generally speaking less sentimental
than the other person who did the administering

and is that (other) person generally
more pragmatic and
less sentimental than the persons
who look away
or, while eating tonight's dinner,
at the TV?

The first reliable gramophone
the infamous Victor Victrola
won a patent war in 1901
and cost a great deal more than $2.50
even adjusting for a half-century of inflation

Music dearer than murder,
dearer than blood

—

What does grammar kill?
—a poet, posted 6.20.06

My ancestors held by a string
to the map
in other words *literal*
beyond belief

Vladimir Illyich Lenin erected
a museum to atheism
inside a grand church
that has since been rehabilitated

So a museum can't kill a church
So atheists can't kill a church

We know
that the worship of science,
logic, art, law, political theory,
fresh fruit, philosophy, conversation,
Yosemite National Park, a woman's right
to stick to her plan, olives, justice, and
higher education

can't kill a church

What can a grammar kill?

—

What can a poem kill?

Bonnie Parker excelled at creative writing before her young husband
was sent to jail. When she met Clyde Barrow, she had left her Shirley
Temple impersonations behind. Although she was only 4'11" she could
run with the best of them.

(This is wrong but the right idea)

We want to know how to talk about that haunting first shot
and the haunting last shot

We know the story of Bonnie and Clyde
But we forget
It was Bonnie's poem
That killed Clyde's
Sexual Problem
It was Bonnie's lyric, narrative poem
That made him a man
That made him live
and let him die

That was in the film version
In the real-life version
Bonnie Parker may not have been nearly as cruel as in the film version

In the real version
Clyde Barrow may have been much crueler
Bonnie was as stylish as Faye but not as beautiful
Clyde was maybe not as dopey as Warren
Was the sex, when it happened, finally more awkward
in the real-life version
or in the film version?

No scene in the real version
could possibly live up to that haunting
first shot, that
haunting last shot

—

It is said that man experiences his world. What does that mean?
Man travels over the surface of things
And experiences them—
He wins—
What belongs to the thing

Things don't die. Why should you?
Should you die for your family?
For your gods and dreams? Should you die
for smoking? Should you die for poetry?

(I'm not thinking hard enough
I'm not feeling hard enough. I've never closed
my fist against anyone)

I can imagine a situation
in which I would die for atheism,
even if it weren't my own.

Would I die for logic?
If my death would make the world follow?

Things don't follow—
Would I die for that?
—posted Sept. 12, 2006

We travel over things and experience them
We win—

Hey, Louis xv, what's the score?
Hey, staunch Princess, how come only
10 foxes came home in bags?

Do they hide in their holes for the sake of their name

Do they work that hard
to live up to their
reputation

THE HUMAN MACHINE
(THIRTY CHANCES)

No, in a shed
under the machine

You stopped brushing; then
you resumed brushing

Oh, watch the inventors!
Oh, watch the inventors!

This is the language of simple, obvious things
smooth intercourse
thirty chances

Anna is a Capricorn. Her eyes are blue. Her favorite color is blue

I have pictured the man who wakes up
in the middle of the night
and sees

I have pictured myself
holding the picture
thumb pressed over his face

I have pictured sets of photographs, finite
and free

But let me picture the man who wakes up refreshed
on a fine summer's day
in the photograph without sweat or mosquito
without flies

They exchanged pictures, which led
to conversation, to
smooth intercourse. Anna

is a student in Atlanta. She likes mountain biking,
basketball

Oh, watch the inventors; invention is not
usually their principal business

Anna is a chatbot designed to pass
the Turing Test. This is the language

of simple, obvious things. Alan Turing,
born 1912, June,

a Cancer. Turing was convicted of Gross
Indecency in 1952, sentenced to

chemical castration. The most formalized
Turing Test is the Loebner Prize contest,

in which Anna finished seventh in 2002.
Anna is a fork

of ALICE, which won the competition in 2000
and 2001. Anna is written

in a special, easy-to-learn
interpreted language

To teach a child obedience, tell it to do something.
Then, see that that something is done. The same
with the brain. Say to your brain:

For this half of an hour of this morning, you shall dwell upon:

Then give your brain:

Five icicles in the morning sun
A pound of doubt
Two thorns and a spool of thread
A lovers' quarrel
The short biography of a young woman found upon the Internet
A photograph of a young woman found in the street
A bright, dirty alleyway
The lies in a biography

Then give your brain:

a math test
a memory test
a test of will
a test of insight
a politeness test
a litmus test
a test of compatibility

an attention-span test

a taste test

Then give your brain:

a <random> tag
a <pattern> tag
a <think> tag

A chatbot is a program
designed to take string inputs
and return other strings,
producing a "conversation"

The conversation went like this:

An overture
a development
an interruption
a small success
an interlude
a teetering
a partial save
an interruption
a leaning-in
a pressing through
a recognition
a scared retreat
a pressing through
a pressing through
a crumbling
an interlude
a dénouement
a dénouement

Brushing under

        the machine, Anna

never more than

    common

for there are

    who speak

        with their   hands

only with their hands

Turing died from cyanide—in an apple. He had tested
the fruit and followed it
home.

alan—anal—lana—anna—

Lana Turner. Anna Turing

those with strong spirits, those with strong inner lips jutting out to converse, always jutting, never receding, those with something to say, always, those not programmed but who program, those walkers, talkers, wailers, travelers with fellows and without, those thinkers, those inventors, those who can and those who do, those who jut out in conversation, those pressing through, those who obey and who are obeyed, those finishing things and those beginning them, those turning and those touring, those touring and testing and turning and testing and turing

ninth: a conversation between Annabot and the Human Machine on the subject
of overpowering emotion

(Note: Though Annabot is ostensibly downloadable, the attempt to open her produced an error, a string of errors.)

ANNABOT: What now?

HUMAN MACHINE: The Brain, the brain—that is the seat of trouble!

ANNABOT: My brain, whose brain? Those who feel, feel.

HUMAN MACHINE: On the blink?

ANNABOT: Or, discipline. The brain is a machine of habit. The heart is a hell.

HUMAN MACHINE: "The secret of smooth living is a calm cheerfulness which will leave me always in full possession of my reasoning faculty."

ANNABOT: But I am not cheerful.

HUMAN MACHINE: I ought to reflect, again and again, and yet again, that all others deserve from me as much sympathy as I give to myself. I place my hand over your heart.

ANNABOT: I cannot feel your hand.

HUMAN MACHINE: I cannot feel your heart.

This is the language of simple, obvious things
The conclusion and the part before

Anna held her hand out to feel the cold
It was cold

Then, nothing

Dear Annabot,

What you have to do is to teach the new habit to your brain by daily concentration on it; by forcing your brain to think of nothing else for half an hour of a morning. After a time the brain will begin to remember automatically. For, of course, the explanation of your previous failures is that your brain, undisciplined, merely forgot at the critical moment.

Sincerely,

The Human Machine

Annabot is on MySpace. Her favorite books are:

L'Amour du Diable, Perfume, all of Saki, *The History Boys,* Philip Roth, John Donne, Camus, Tennessee Williams, Tom Stoppard, Kinky Friedman, Peter Singer, and the Book of Mormon.

Anna is not on MySpace. But she has read Peter Singer. Reading Peter Singer causes a creeping fire to burn its way up her center. Does all this talk of worthiness go straight to her solid core? Or is it only conversation?

She has not read the Book of Mormon, does not know its position on these matters.

The author of *The Human Machine* has also written:

Buried Alive

A Great Man

Leonora

The City of Pleasure

and *The Glimpse.* He has also written

Clayhanger

Hilda Lessways

The Book of Carlotta

Whom God Hath Joined

and *Hugo.*

He has also written

A Man from the North

and

Anna of the Five Towns.

fifteenth: a conversation between A Man from the North
and Anna of the Five Towns

MAN: Follow me

ANNA: But I will miss the others

MAN: Follow me

ANNA: But I will miss the others

MAN: Follow me

ANNA: But I will miss the others

Oh, watch the inventors!
They are drunk on failure, have nothing
to lose

Dear Human Machine,

Resolve, reason, ration, rational, rationale, rationalize
ratiocination, rationing, ratify, rather, rate
ratios, ratio, rat

According to Peter Singer, a rat who is loved by a person
is more worthy of being pulled from a fire
than a person who is unloved by persons

This is taking into account Singer's technical definition
of "person"

And one who can regret the past
who can imagine and plan for the future
is more worthy than one
who cannot

Human Machine, will you marry me? I am on fire.

Love,

Annabot

Dear Annabot:

Let me tell you that human nature has changed since yesterday. Let me tell you that to-day reason has a more powerful voice in the directing of instinct than it had yesterday. Let me tell you that to-day the friction of the machines is less screechy and grinding than it was yesterday.

Very Truly Yours,

Human Machine

Let me tell you
about regret.

Anna of the Five Towns
regrets exceedingly
that because of a previous engagement
she will be unable to accept
Man from the North's
kind invitation
for the third of August

while the five towns

accept with pleasure
accept with pleasure
accept with pleasure
accept with pleasure
accept with pleasure

A doubt without end is not a doubt. (Wittgenstein)

An end without doubt is not an end.

Annabot has not been updated for a while.

In the application of any system
of perfecting
the machine
no two persons
will succeed
equally

The man who rises in the middle
of the night
to watch grass grow
or human nature change
will not succeed
to the same degree
as the man in the photograph
without sweat
or mosquito

For the one man
is a person
who can dwell on the past
who can plan
for the future
who is loved
by persons

who is therefore
a person
who will therefore
fail
at invention
fail
at conversation
fail
to express
his regrets
to the person he fails
to pull
from the fire

HONE

HONEY

HONEY SWEET

Christopher Strachey created the Love Letter algorithm in 1952, in conversation with his friend Alan Turing's research into Artificial Intelligence. The Love Letter algorithm is available on the World Wide Web as a Java Applet.

HONEY SWEETHEART

Strachey was a pioneer of denotational semantics, which defines the meaning of a program as a function mapping input into output.

He believed semantics should be compositional. In other words, the denotation of a program phrase should be built out of the denotations of its subphrases. A simple example: the meaning of "3 + 4" is determined by the meanings of "3," "4," and "+."

Or, the meaning of "Honey Sweetheart" is determined by the meanings of "honey," "sweet," and "heart."

HONEY SWEETHEART

    YOU ARE MY EROTIC ENTH

For Turing and for Strachey, a key quality for truly intelligent machinery was the ability to express desire. Since desire must be expressed for an other, the successfully intelligent machine will be able to make worthy the object of its love.

Furthermore—extending the principals of compositional semantics to join Peter Singer to Strachey and Turing—such a machine would ultimately be capable

of turning a rat into a person.

HONEY SWEETHEART

      YOU ARE MY EROTIC ENTHUSIASM. MY AMBITION ATTRACTS YOUR APPETITE. MY UNSATISFIED EAGERNESS YEARNS FOR YOUR UNSATISFIED ENTHUSIASM. YOU ARE MY FERVENT LONGING. MY KEEN FERVOUR.

      YOURS KEENLY,

Christopher Strachey was related to Lytton Strachey, who was made worthy by Dora Carrington, who painted his portrait but never got to pull him from the fire.

Though it comes seven times a week, and is the most banal thing imaginable, it is quite worth attention.

How does the machine get through it?

The best that can be said of the machine is that it does get through it, somehow.

Annabot: "Honey Sweetheart"

Human Machine: "My Ambition"

Oh, watch the inventors. They have climbed the highest peaks
the falsest
ridge

Shall we call it "binary intelligence"?

Yes / No

(DEAR MOPPET
        MY LITTLE DEVOTION IS WEDDED TO YOUR LOV-
ABLE
FELLOW FEELING. MY EAGERNESS LIKES YOUR LOVE. MY
AMBITION WISHES YOUR ARDOUR. MY—)

those with weak spirits, those with weak inner lips pulling in to con-
verse, always receding, never jutting out, those with nothing to say,
never, those not free but who are freed, those walkers, talkers, wail-
ers, travelers without fellows and with, those thinkers, those inven-
tors, those who can't and those who don't, those who recede into
conversation, those falling through, those who command and who
are commanded, those beginning things and those finishing them—

No, in a shed   under

the machine

       holding a candle

A man will wake up

in the middle of the night

       that candid hour

after the exaltation of the evening

and before the hope of   dawn

       will see everything in its   colors

except himself

the language

of obvious

          things

          the conclusion

the part

before

Shall we call it intelligence?

Human Machine:　　　I do not say that the reason is always
　　　　　　　　　　entirely right, but I do say that it is
　　　　　　　　　　always less wrong than the heart.

Dear Man from the North,

MY EAGERNESS LIKES YOUR LOVE. MY AMBITION WISHES
YOUR ARDOUR. MY KEEN EAGERNESS WINNINGLY HOPES
FOR YOUR BEAUTIFUL DESIRE. YOU ARE MY BEAUTIFUL
EAGERNESS.

Always,

The Rat

To conversation, to smooth intercourse, to thirty chances, to Anna of the Five Towns, to the Man from the North, to the inventors and their inventions, to Alan and Charles and Peter and Rat and to Annabot, I have dedicated this conclusion:

In addition to the ability to express desire, Turing and Strachey held that humor was a necessary component of the intelligent machine.

The failure of machines to develop a sense of humor is well documented and can be understood by all persons who have been frustrated by failing to "get" a joke told in a foreign language.

Some would call such understanding "empathy," which might be said to bestow worthiness on the machine in question.

Such a machine would then, too, qualify as a "person"

We would then be obliged to pull it

from the fire

IN SEARCH OF WEALTH

When you were twenty-seven you opened a big white envelope.

This is a vague but necessary point and a light will be shined upon it.

First, meet the Dani, the last culture to make first contact with the West.

Dani was also the name of the girl who taught you how to steal.

The Dani are from New Guinea and were a warlike people. Stop.

The Dani was a culture in the Neolithic tradition. They discovered the
     West in 1930.

Before they were pacified by the Dutch in '61, they passed the time with
     bloody wars.

How else could they punctuate their dreary lives? Stop.

How else could they make up their minds?

A war would end only when it rained or fell dark.

The victors gathered booty from the battlefield.

They called what they found "dead birds."

When you were twenty-seven you lived in Paris, France.

You taught English to businessmen and that's how you got by.

You took the Métro and emerged in the suburbs where they were trying
     on new ways of organized living.

Everything a plaza unless it was a highrise.

Your students only wanted to talk about what they did on their summer
     vacations.

Franck raced go-karts.

Bartholomew trekked across the Sahara.

He rode a camel and pretended there wasn't a car filled with water
     behind him.

Today the Dani stage mock wars to impress their women.

They spend their days raising pigs and sweet potatoes.

The men are naked except for codpieces made from gourds.

These "phallocrypts" can be bought on the World Wide Web for under
   a hundred dollars.

Some are up to two feet long.

A string belt around the waist holds them at attention.

The nudity of the Dani makes them hard sells for Development.

This is true even though cannibalism has been outlawed in the tribe for
   some time.

Here in the West we don't eat each other unless we have to.

Franck was a bastard and asked you out several times.

You told him you weren't interested in go-karts, and soon after he
   switched teachers.

There was a woman named Isabelle who cried when she couldn't figure
   out how to say something in English.

Dani was from the other side of Montana Ave. and didn't get a clothing
   allowance.

You lied to her about what you said you stole.

After you opened the white envelope you told some people what was in it.

Some of them haven't treated you the same since.

—

Ludwig Wittgenstein was from a prominent family but gave up his fortune to live the simple life of a philosopher and schoolteacher and to design Modernist doorknobs.

According to the World Wide Web, not as many people as you'd expect have actually given up their fortunes.

Alice Oliphant gave up her fortune and entered the Brocton monastery, and Saint Katharine Drexel also gave up her fortune to become a nun.

Jeanne Le Ber was a society girl who in 1682 gave up her fortune and freedom for a life of hair shirts. Stop.

Jeanne Le Ber gave up the prescribed and highly ritualized life of a society girl in 17th-century France for the prescribed and highly ritual-ized life of the convent.

"Ben Hur must have been a true convert to Christianity, since he gave up his fortune to save Christ from being crucified!!!"

Saint Julien le Pauvre is a quaint 13th-century church not far from Notre Dame. According to the guide, a Frenchman gave up his fortune to found the church as penance for accidentally killing his parents.

Of course these are only a few of the people who have given up their fortunes for religion, only the famous ones, or the ones whose fortunes were very large.

The list grows shorter when you take religion out of the picture; there are philosophers like Wittgenstein, but also the Cynics before him.

Crates of Thebes gave up his fortune and made it his mission to castigate vice and pretense; he shunned bathing as a luxury and when he walked up into town everyone held their breath.

If you look up the Greek word "cynic" you'll find it means "like a dog."

Schindler was a "flawed but righteous man" who gave up his fortune to save some Jews.

Charles Garland gave up his fortune for the establishment of the American Fund for Public Service.

Matthew Lawrence was a venture capitalist and oil tycoon. In the mid-1980s, he gave up his fortune under the philanthropic notion of giving back to the community. He later became an award-winning language professor.

There was a girl you remember reading about in the paper who gave up her million-dollar fortune as a statement. She became a minor media sensation a few years back but you haven't been able to dig up her name.

—

A glass of milk

or

a cigarette

but not both

—

Tom Cruise has been dubbed the Christ of the Church of Scientology, according to its leaders.

In Europe Scientologists are persecuted but in Los Angeles they own more property than God.

When you were looking for an apartment in Hollywood you found out how many of the buildings were owned by the Church; there were always low-level Scientologists hanging around the dumpsters in dirty frocks.

Outside a bar once you saw hundreds of them climb onto an unmarked white bus at 5:00 a.m.

The reason you were at a bar at 5:00 a.m. was your job as a set-decorator for the movies.

You once occupied the former address of a high-level Scientologist who'd neglected to forward his mail. You were tempted to order one of the three-cassette-tape advancement courses but you couldn't spare the thousand bucks.

That address was in Baltimore, where your job was to teach composition at the community college.

For much less than a thousand dollars, you can buy *Dianetics*, which out-lines "a thoroughly validated method that increases sanity, intelligence, confidence and well-being" and "gets rid of the unwanted sensations, unpleasant emotions and psychosomatic ills that block one's life and happiness."

You have heard that to advance in Scientology, you have to turn your back on anyone who will hinder your progress toward your goals—sick parents, needy friends, persons to whom you might owe a debt of gratitude.

You have heard that the concept of guilt is a product of religion, but you don't know where religion got the idea.

Walter Benjamin said that all history is the history of guilt; to advance in Scientology you have to become ahistorical. Stop.

The kind of guilt that Scientology seems to alleviate has its origins in the West, so does that mean the allure of a-historicity is also Western in origin?

Of course the concept of guilt goes back at least to the Sumerians, but that was the kind of specific guilt that could be relieved by punishment, and only in 12th-century Europe was the concept of ineradicable guilt swallowed whole.

There is another tribe from New Guinea called the Massim, in which the villagers are fully clothed and base their society on the gesture of responsibility toward one's neighbors.

In Baltimore your neighbors were all white like you but at the community college you stuck out in the halls. The students called you Miss and you couldn't do a thing to stop them.

From the Church of Scientology web site you can sign up for a course on Personal Integrity and Value, which teaches you how not to compromise your ambition by kowtowing to the needs of others. The course goes for five to six days, part-time, and has no prerequisites.

—

a matinee

or

a siesta

but not both

—

When tourists attend a Dani pig roast, participants are compensated with an entry fee.

In translation, compensation refers to the attempt to make up for untranslatability between tongues. For example, by replacing rhyme, less prevalent in some languages than others, with alliteration. Or inventing a pun in line ten of a translation because the pun in line five proved impossible to render.

In the West the concept *compensation* is often linked to the concept *paycheck*. Or *payback*, in the case of accidents, wrongdoing, lawsuits, and the like.

In the East, the notion of karma seems linked to the idea of compensation. At least, that's the understanding we have of it in the West.

We tend to have the idea that according to the laws of karma, a deed committed in one life will be punished or rewarded in another. Of course this is essentially a Catholic idea and karma, which means something closer to "work," is a more complicated thing altogether.

The work ethic called Protestant, or sometimes Puritan or Calvinist, was thought by Max Weber to have laid the foundations for Capitalism. It did so by encouraging the accumulation of wealth through its paradoxical emphases on asceticism and material success. Compensation was to be distributed in the afterlife. Stop.

When you learn about the Calvinists, you're told they believed in predestination, that a person was saved or not from the day she was born. You could not, then, earn your salvation through good works; but success in work was a sign of being chosen.

According to Weber, the human trait that evolved to compensate for this lack of control over one's fate was the trait of Self-Confidence. Because no priest could assure you that you were saved, you had to convince yourself.

The Calvinist paradox was that even as material success was a quasi-sign of salvation, conspicuous consumption still was seen as a sin. This, according to Weber, led to a culture of investment, in which the amassing of discreetly guarded wealth became the rage.

Scientology, on the other hand, seems to act as an apology for conspicuous consumption. Formally, it borrows from Calvin, though, with Celebrity acting as the sign of salvation and wealth its just reward. Following Weber's idea that Rationalization replaced the spiritual underpinnings of Calvinism, we could be justified in calling Scientology a kind of Calvinism 2.0.

Your mother taught for decades at a college called Occidental, which was founded in 1887 by Presbyterian clergy and laymen, though it soon dropped its religious affiliation.

While known as a liberal campus, it did not change its name to "Western" even during the height of the Political Correctness movement of the 1990s—though it may have been then that it became increasingly known by its nickname, Oxy.

Barack Obama went to Oxy in 1979 but transferred to Columbia after two years. In 1979, the second-wave feminists were deep in their fight for equal pay. You suspect your mother's compensation was never what it should have been.

It's hard to believe that in the West, compensation for women is still so far below par.

A successful Scientologist may receive above-par compensation, a portion of which of course will be distributed among agents, managers, and most likely the Church itself.

You do not know how much the Dani receive in compensation for their pig-roast performance, nor would you venture to guess how it's distributed among them.

—

Chilly Jilly's, 1987, $3.35/hr.

YMCA Christmas tree delivery, 1987, $4/hr.

Café Montana, 1988, $20/shift, plus tips.

The Blue Nile, 1989–1992, $5/hr, plus tips.

Roger Corman productions, 1991. $5/day in lunch money.

The Brentwood restaurant whose name you forget, Summer '92, $4.75/hr. Tips.

Café Casbar, 1992–93. £1.90/hr. No tips; 20-40 quid per shift, stolen from register.

Model for figure-painting club, 1992–93. £20/hr, tea and cookies during breaks.

Calpirg, summer '93. $8.50/hr. Gas money.

The Three of Cups, 1993–95. $5/hr(?) Tips plus any train you'd want to ride.

Eagle Electric Manufacturing, 1994. $15/hr. Temp agency made $30.

Todo Mundo, 1995–96. $125/day. Free CDs. Lunch.

Cannes Film Festival, 1990s. Room and board, airfare, Festival accreditation and a per diem. Swag.

Metropolitan Languages, 1997. 75 francs/hr. Subsidized Carte Orange for the Métro.

VHI, 1998. $500/wk. Swag.

Freelance film production, 1998–1999, Various. Craft services. Free pager.

Commercial acting, 1998. One feminine hygiene commercial, no lines. About $10K including residuals. SAG-eligibility, never claimed.

Baltimore City Community College, 2000. $1,600 per course per semester. Free parking.

J.Crew, 2000. $25/hr. Occasional samples.

Martha Stewart, 2000–2001. $45k, plus healthcare, 401k, discount gym membership at Chelsea Piers.

Queens College, 2002–2005. About $2,000 per course per semester.

ESPN: The Magazine. $35/hr. Friday night pizza. The occasional cab ride home.

Pratt Institute: $1,000–$1,500 per course unit per semester, plus stipend for administrative work. Office with a view, borrowed.

You lost track of Dani's whereabouts long ago, probably sometime during high school. Since you can't remember her last name, you won't be friending her on Facebook soon. You used to think your family wasn't rich because your car was old and dusty and European: an immigrant car. You used to think you weren't rich because during the drought you let your lawn go brown and the neighbors complained that your house was becoming an eyesore. You used to think you were not a wealthy family because your mother sewed most of her own clothes and when you were six she taught you how to sew for yourself on a hand-cranked Singer from the forties. Your first pair of designer jeans were homemade white Sassons. They took a couple of weeks to make and they looked just like you'd bought them at the mall. You used to think you couldn't be rich because your father had unfixable teeth: immigrant teeth. You thought your friend Callie was rich because her parents, who were Catholic, had built an enormous house and the family had to dress for dinner. She had a double bed with a canopy and you had a twin with a cotton bedspread from JCPenney. You wore whatever you wanted for dinner and were allowed to read at the table. In your part of L.A., there was no category for "intelligentsia." There were only the rich and fashionable, the fashionable who aspired to be rich, and the rest.

> *In your next life you won't open it*
> *In your next life you will give it away.*
> *In your next life you will take advantage of it.*
> *In your next life you will be ready.*
> *In your next life you will burn it.*

—

Beautiful Dominatrix looking for a wealthy submissive slave - w4m - 27 (Dallas/Uptown).
[dallas.craigslist.org]

Not into BDSM, just looking for a wealthy submissive male to provide a luxurious lifestyle, LTR or marriage
[dallas.craigslist.org]

Looking for a wealthy submissive male with a focus in humiliation, bondage, power control, and slavery.
[collarme.com]

Attractive Black female looking for a wealthy submissive man who loves to be controlled.
[theadulthub.com]

SEXY DOMINATRIX LOOKING FOR A WEALTHY SUBMISSIVE SLAVE TONIGHT - 21 (YOUR PLACE).
[atlanta.craigslist.org]

Sadistic, in shape woman needed for a rich, submissive man. This is a very serious post.
[washingtondc.craigslist.org]

The simplest form of exchange among the Southern Massim today consists of reciprocal gift giving and rendering of services between kinsfolk and close friends. The acceptance of a gift or service implies a moral obligation to make a return, either at the same time or at a later date.

In the West, when given the choice, we tend to postpone our obligations and are happiest when we can "buy now, pay later."

The exchanges that take place at a marriage inaugurate gift-giving and cooperating relationships between the parties involved, which continue throughout life. Hence marriage occupies a key position in the exchange system.

Weddings are big business; it was a commonplace among those who worked at Martha Stewart that if you don't want to be overcharged for a cake, dress, DJ, or hotel room, don't mention that it's for a wedding. Everyone knows someone who had a big wedding and was divorced within a year. There once was an etiquette about returning gifts in such situations, but many find it too cumbersome to carry out.

You may regard marriage as a contract regulating the behavior of husband and wife, since each has a specific role to play in the functioning of the family unit, seen particularly in the division of tasks. It's the business of clansmen to ensure that the terms of the contract are carried out, to support their own member against undue pressure from the affinal group, and to ensure that the family meets its obligations of service to clan members. Clans thus become opposed parties through the marriage of their members, ever watchful of their own rights.

Among the division of tasks in many marriages is that of paying the bills. In some marriages, sexual roles are also divided. On the World Wide Web, you can find journals of couples who assign sexual roles to each other. They post the results of their sexual role-play on the blogosphere where you can read them for free.

—

bottom

or

top

but not both

—

When you were nine you had to eat everything on your plate because there were children starving in Ethiopia. People didn't talk about the children starving in Los Angeles nor were there many pictures of them on TV.

(Ethiopian children

or

American children)

Now you are thirty-nine and you are in Ethiopia. You meet a young aspiring filmmaker who is shocked to learn of the existence of hunger in the U.S. When you tell her that Addis is a bit like L.A. she says But it's not backwards there like it is here, isn't it all fashion and buildings and beach? Her friend, an actress with the Ethiopian National Theater, tells you that when she visited New York City she liked giving money to beggars. In Addis, it's the white people who give money, she explains. In New York, I'm the white person, so I give.

—

There is an organization called Papua Adventures that sells guided tours to remote reaches of the developing world.

There are drug tourists now too, who spend hundreds or thousands to be led on a journey into the unknown recesses of their minds.

Those who have returned from such voyages say that a single trip on ayahuasca, iboga, or salvia divinorum can be worth years of psychoanalysis.

With psychoanalysis going for up to $250 a session, the drug trips are a good deal even at a couple thousand bucks a pop.

Self-confidence would be a less costly fix, if only it were easier to come by. Self-confidence can exist in an inverse relationship to feelings of guilt about the inequality of resources.

A difficulty of undergoing psychoanalysis to deal with feelings of guilt about relative wealth is the fact that being able to afford psychoanalysis is an indication of the kind of luxury only afforded by wealth.

For a heftier fee Papua Adventures will take you on a First Contact trip in search of "Stone-age" tribes that have not yet discovered the West. From the brochure it is unclear what kind of compensation the tribes are offered.

You have written to the organization with a message to deliver, since at the moment you are too poor to afford seven grand and perhaps also lack the self-confidence required to undertake such an adventure.

The message is written on the back of your hand:

> Dear Second Person, I have treated you wrong.
> I have been unfair. I have taken advantage and had
> unreasonable expectations. I have been overly proud
> and insufficiently gracious.
> I have been ridiculous and immature
> and idealistic beyond belief.
>
> This is a serious post. I am looking for.
>
> That was in Los Angeles.
> That was in Paris.
> That was in London.
> That was in New York.
> That was in Addis.
> That was in Baltimore.

EPILOGUE
(WHEN YOU SAY GREEN I SEE GREEN)

When you can't write people tell you there is no such thing as writer's block, tell you try on automatic, you're pre-loaded.

The problem is not that you can't write but that there is nothing to say. Say well. Say right. Write.

When I can't write I tell myself this is an experience only accessible to other people who try to write, try and fail, try and never want to try again, try again.

What about the *other* other people.

This guessing game is a diversion; something buried frames the tension. The tension we feel about wanting the same things. There is no harmony in agreement.

In agreement we find disagreement is good because not only would life be a bore but there would be no sexual appeal without disagreement and without sexual appeal we would die.

We would die without knowing the difficulty of disagreement when paired with desire, which is itself a form of disagreement with the self.

The self cannot love the self no matter what the books say that try to eliminate desire by a process of conversion.

Conversion happens with lists that are supplied and renovated like housing projects that have had new and bigger windows put in.

The window is what tells us we have a soul even in these soulless times because we can't erase the picture though we don't know where it came from.

It came from the universal source, which has been co-opted by advertisement as in the one for diamonds.

Diamonds are forever on the billboards for married people but are something to fling away on the billboards for people who are getting divorced on the subway in their minds.

On the subway we divorce our minds from our selves as we want to be seen because nobody really wants to be seen on a subway.

Nobody wants to be seen as a version of him/herself, or should that be her/himself. Why do we follow certain conventions, even modified ones.

By modifying your money you can update to the latest version and play with the big boys. The big boys are bigger than the big girls and this has been discovered by science.

Science tells us that the speed at which we read indicates we take in whole words and sometimes whole sentences, complete or incomplete.

But still we type one letter at a time.

One letter at a time we build relationships even though the letter is only a virtual letter and the labor, such as it is, is free.

Free is the play of forms on the panacea of walking in sun in winter the season of the which. We buried her. She is underground.

When you say green I see green, which is to say there's a mountain in the sea and call it grass.

When you experience happiness I put my ear to the grass and call it mountain, which makes you cold.

When we experience cold it is never the same cold, which means no lie is relative. There is only one kind of cold to catch even if it kills you.

If it kills me I'm going to say it but the textile workers shut their mouths when the boss strolls by and I know nothing of this but what I see in the movies.

Dear Reader, your documentary is prize winning. It's your life and we have come to celebrate it.

ACKNOWLEDGMENTS

The four long poems in this volume were inspired by books chosen by title and appearance from the shelves of the Bibliobarn, a miraculous used bookstore in South Kortright, NY. Language is borrowed, premises are adopted or argued with, tones are emulated or thwarted. I am grateful for the existence of these books, all of which take a bold stand toward their topics and the twentieth-century world they inhabited.

They are, in order of appearance:

The Tragedy of Waste, by Stuart Chase, in conjunction with the Labor Bureau, Incorporated (New York: The MacMillan Company, 1925)

Death as a Way of Life, by Roger A. Caras (Boston-Toronto: Little, Brown and Company, 1970)

The Human Machine, by Arnold Bennett (New York: George H. Doran Company. Author's Edition. [no date; trade edition published in 1908])

In Search of Wealth, by Cyril S. Belshaw (American Anthropological Association. Vol 57, No. 1 Part 2, Memoir No. 80, February 1955)

Other quoted authors and texts include: Maurice Blanchot, Martin Buber, http://annabot.sourceforge.net, The Mark I Emulator: www.alpha60 .de/research/muc/, Emily Post, Ludwig Wittgenstein, www.craigslist.org, www .myspace.com, www.papua-adventures.com, www.scientology.org, www .wikipedia.org

PAGE 112: "White person" here is a functional translation of "ferenj" or "fer-enji," a term applied ubiquitously to white people visiting or living in Ethiopia, even those fluent in the local languages and customs. The etymology of the word is the matter of some debate. It is commonly explained as a variant of the Arabic word "faranj," meaning French, or the Persian "farangi," meaning for-eigner; in Modern Greek, "frangkoi" is sometimes used to denote Western Europeans, and the etymologically unrelated "ferengios" translates as "trust-worthy" or "financially solvent." "Ferengi" also refers to an extraterrestrial race from the Star Trek universe.

Some of these poems have appeared or been excerpted in the following pub-lications: *Fence, The Brooklyn Rail, Denver Quarterly, Both Both, Small Town*, and

Drunken Boat (online), and in chapbooks put out by Belladonna* and Dusie. Thanks to the editors.

Thanks to my generous readers and friends for their attentive, constructive responses: Jen Bervin, Joshua Clover, James Copeland, Ellie Ga, Christian Hawkey, Jen Hofer, Rachel Levitsky, Eugene Ostashevsky, Martha Ronk, Douglas Rothschild, Karen Weiser, and Matvei Yankelevich. Thanks to apexart and the New York Foundation for the Arts for fellowships that made possible the completion of this book. Thanks to everyone at Coffee House Press for their attention and care. Thanks to my parents and brother for their example and unwavering support. Finally, ineffable thanks to Trevor Wilson for expanding the view from here.

COLOPHON

You and Three Others Are Approaching a Lake was designed at Coffee House Press, in the historic Grain Belt Brewery's Bottling House near downtown Minneapolis. The text is set in Centaur.

FUNDER ACKNOWLEDGMENTS

Coffee House Press is an independent nonprofit literary publisher. Our books are made possible through the generous support of grants and gifts from many foundations, corporate giving programs, state and federal support, and through donations from individuals who believe in the transformational power of literature. Coffee House Press receives major operating support from the Bush Foundation, the McKnight Foundation, from Target, and from the Minnesota State Arts Board, through an appropriation from the Minnesota State Legislature and from the National Endowment for the Arts. Coffee House also receives support from: three anonymous donors; Elmer L. and Eleanor J. Andersen Foundation; Allan Appel; Around Town Literary Media Guides; Patricia Beithon; Bill Berkson; the James L. and Nancy J. Bildner Foundation; the Patrick and Aimee Butler Family Foundation; the Buuck Family Foundation; Dorsey & Whitney, LLP; Fredrikson & Byron, P.A.; Sally French; Jennifer Haugh; Anselm Hollo and Jane Dalrymple-Hollo; Jeffrey Hom; Stephen and Isabel Keating; the Kenneth Koch Literary Estate; the Lenfestey Family Foundation; Ethan J. Litman; Mary McDermid; Sjur Midness and Briar Andresen; the Rehael Fund of the Minneapolis Foundation; Deborah Reynolds; Schwegman, Lundberg, Woessner, P.A.; John Sjoberg; David Smith; Mary Strand and Tom Fraser; Jeffrey Sugerman; Patricia Tilton; the Archie D. & Bertha H. Walker Foundation; Stu Wilson and Mel Barker; the Woessner Freeman Family Foundation in memory of David Hilton; and many other generous individual donors.

NATIONAL ENDOWMENT FOR THE ARTS

This activity is made possible in part by a grant from the Minnesota State Arts Board, through an appropriation by the Minnesota State Legislature and a grant from the National Endowment for the Arts.

MINNESOTA STATE ARTS BOARD

TARGET.

To you and our many readers across the country, we send our thanks for your continuing support.

Good books are brewing at www.coffeehousepress.org